BEING MORTAL

Illness, Medicine, and What Matters in the End

Executive Summary

Book§Swift

Other Books by Book§Swift

Methodology

In producing these Executive Summaries, the Book§Swift team dedicates a researcher, writer and editor to the task of summarizing the key points from each chapter. The writer is then tasked with creating a master list of the key points. Further analysis of the book is then undertaken by the writer to extract the key concepts and golden nuggets that are to be presented in a concise and easily understood manner. The Book§Swift team strives diligently to allow readers to digest the Executive Summary in minimal time and walk away with the key concepts.

Once the first draft has been written, the initial team individually reviews and revises the Executive Summary to enhance value by eliminating excess information which detracts from conveying the key concepts. To ensure our Executive Summaries capture the golden nuggets and key concepts as intended, we review and study extra sources such as summaries, briefs, other texts, and interviews with the author.

Why an Executive Summary?

Time is the most scarce and important resource we have in this life and so we at Book§Swift strongly believe we should maximize this resource to its greatest potential, day in and day out. Being avid readers and writers, we have created these summaries not only for ourselves as there are only so many books that we are able to read at a time (some in our team even read a book a day!), but we have also created these Executive Summaries for those of you who simply don't have the time to get through every single page of 200-500 page book, word for word.

We aim to provide you the opportunity to read and gain the information from books in the shortest amount of time possible enabling you to live a better life and be of even greater value to society which ultimately benefits everyone. People who regularly read will also gain value as they will be able to refresh themselves on the main ideas or subtleties they may have missed from their first read through of the book.

The biggest pet peeve we have with books is that the majority of them are simply packed with an intense amount of filler, hence our name Book§Summaries Without Incessant Filler Traps. Our Executive Summaries solve this issue by having no fluff as we cut straight to the point without losing the key message, so that you may immediately benefit from the knowledge and information by applying it into your life in the shortest amount of time possible.

CONTENTS

INTRODUCTION

Atul Gawande started his medical career and learnt as most medical students do. They learned about anatomy and physiology by deconstructing the human body, and were introduced to the limitless discoveries that have accumulated in medicine over the past century to prevent death. One thing they weren't taught however was how they should deal with the death, decline, and mortality of their patients. They weren't taught about what a person might desire or want as they aged, and they certainly weren't told how this might affect them or their caregivers in the end. Medical school teaches students how to save lives by finding the correct solutions, it doesn't teach students how to deal with mortality.

In fact, Gawande only remembers one instance during his medical schooling where the topic of death and mortality was broached. It was during discussions of a fictional character in Leo Tolstoy's novella, The Death of Ivan Illyich. The character in the story was evidently dying as he gradually became more and more frail over time, the numerous doctors that diagnosed his unknown disease kept treating him with remedies that had no effect. The dying man's family and doctors strongly believed he was simply ill, and was not dying. In the end, the man simply wanted to be pitied and comforted in the fact that he was dying despite those close to him disagreeing, this included the doctors who strongly avoided touching on this subject. The students, along with Gawande figured that in today's day and age they most likely could have cured him, but also would've been compassionate, comforting and sympathetic towards the man in their role as a doctor.

Gawande recalls a story of a patient he dealt with in his junior surgical residency. The patient had lost his wife to cancer years earlier when she ended up in intensive care, strapped to a ventilator. At that point in time, the patient expressed to his son a strong desire that if he were found in the same situation he would rather die than lose his independence and need to be taken care of. A few years later, the patient was diagnosed with cancer that was incurable and was posed with two treatment options. The first would be comfort care which he strongly attested, and the second option was surgery that would not cure him or reverse his inevitable paralysis. The patient chose the surgical option.

The surgery was a technical success but resulted in the patient entering intensive care as he developed an infection that would continue to worsen until fourteen days later when the patient would be taken off life support by Gawande. What struck Gawande the most from his experience with this patient was that the doctors knew that even if the surgery was a success, it would not have given the patient his life back. The surgery would have only provided him at best, a measure of some semblance of life for a few more weeks before the cancer would ultimately end up taking him. The doctors did not even discuss this ultimatum with the patient because they "fix problems", they don't deal with frailty and end of life issues. So Gawande pondered whether these doctors were worse off or better than the doctors depicted in Tolstoy's novella?

People today live longer lives than ever before in history. Unfortunately the medical profession has not prepared for this reality even though scientific advances have turned the processes of aging and dying into medical experiences. In 1945 most deaths occurred at home and by the 1980's this fell to only 17%, and of those that passed away, the majority had sudden deaths or were located in areas to secluded to be able to receive any medical attention. The entire industrialized world has shifted the experience of advanced aging and death onto hospitals and nursing homes, and the evidence shows that this approach is failing.

We have allowed our fates to be controlled by the imperatives of medicine, technology, and strangers in nursing homes or hospitals. Rather than providing people facing their mortality the things that matter most to them in life, we have provided them with treatments that confuse their brains and weaken their bodies for a slight chance of benefit. Our reluctance to examine what it means to age, become frail and experience death has made thing worse than they ought to be. Gawande wrote Being Mortal to understand what has occurred and developed over the past few decades in the hopes that changes can be made to the current approach of mortality.

1 – THE INDEPENDENT SELF

As Gawande grew up he never witnessed serious illness or the difficulties of old age. That was until he was in college and began dating the woman who would become his wife, Kathleen. Kathleen's grandmother, Alice Hobson was seventy-seven when Gawande first met her. She lived alone in her house and drove a big V8 Chevy Impala. She cooked for herself, delivered meals on wheels, went to the gym, and even fixed her own plumbing and mowed her own yard.

When Gawande's father first met Alice, his father was surprised she actually lived alone. His father was an urologist that grew up in India before coming to America for residency training. The cultural norm in India was for the family to take in their elderly and care for them until their death. During Gawande's father's residency training, he embraced the American culture, met his wife, became an American citizen, and sent money back home to his family in India whom took care of his elderly father Sitaram Gawande. The only aspect he did not embrace of American culture was how the elderly were treated. From his perspective, if they elderly did not already have serious needs, they were bound to develop them and strongly felt it should be the family's responsibility to take the aged in, give them company, and look after them. The thought of the elderly spending their last conscious moments surrounded by nurses and doctors who barely knew their names bothered Gawande's father.

Sitaram Gawande, Gawande's grandfather, had a traditional old age as one would have in India. Sitaram was a farmer in a village called Uti, where his ancestors had cultivated land for centuries and was revered not in spite of his age but because of it. He was consulted on important decisions, such as marriages, business problems, and land issues. Needless to say, Sitaram held a place of high honor in the family and within the community even as Sitaram was more than a 100 years old.

In America, Sitaram would have most likely been placed in a nursing home at his age as he would not have been defined as a person having the ability to operate at a functional level. Health professionals have provided classifications for functional levels of a person to determine whether they could safely live by themselves. The Eight Activities of Daily Living are classified as without assistance, the ability to: eat, use the toilet, bathe, dress, groom, get out of bed, get out of a chair and walk. If you can't shop for yourself, make your own food, do your own housekeeping, do your laundry, manage your medications, use the phone, travel on your own, or handle your own finances - the Eight Independent Activities of Daily Living - then you are classed as not having the ability to live on your own safely.

Sitaram could only perform some of these activities without assistance, but in India as his family took care of him with someone always nearby at all times, he never went without help or assistance of some sort. His family made it possible for him to continue to live his life the way he wanted to, until he died at the age of 109 as he fell and hit his head walking off a bus.

For most of history those who reached old age were treated much like

Sitaram Gawande was, usually with the youngest daughter staying at home to take care of their parents till they passed away. Back then old age was a rarity and was actually revered in societies, people who reached old age generally served a special purpose as guardians of tradition, knowledge, and history. So much respect was given to the elderly that people would pretend to be older than they were, not younger, when giving their age as studies have shown that in past censuses people used to overstate their age. In today's day and age, people often understate their age.

In 1790, people aged sixty-five and older accounted for 2% of the population. This percentage has now increased to 14% and old age no longer holds the value of rarity it once had, also with advances in technologies, the value in the wisdom and knowledge of the elderly has also declined. Over time, the children that once stayed at home to care for their parents have left, followed their own dreams and gotten their own jobs and families. Parents have not been upset by this change however as they've found that they could stop working till old age and the concept of "retirement" had arrived allowing the elderly to stop working, and take time out for themselves.

As life expectancy increased, the size of families decreased and the age that couples stopped having children also decreased. With better nutrition, sanitation, and medical care, people continued to live even longer. Parents could see their children reach adulthood and had plenty of time to worry about old age. When the elderly had the financial means, they would actually choose what social scientists have deemed "intimacy at a distance" which was to live in separate households form their children. In the early-twentieth-century America, 60% of those over the age of sixty-five resided with a child, by 1975 this percentage had dropped to below 15% and this pattern has been recognized worldwide. Over the past few decades, the choices that the elderly have had have proliferated and this shows tremendous signs of progress in aged care.

In 1960, Sun City was launched by Del Webb who popularized the term "retirement community" where the elderly could live together at their leisure. They could play golf, visit a shopping arcade, a recreation center and most of all, the community offered camaraderie with others similar in age to dine and participate in other activities with. Even though this concept was a controversial idea at the time, the concept proved to be massively popular with the adoption of it throughout Europe, the Americas, and even Asia. The veneration of elders may have disappeared, however this was not due to the veneration of youth. It was because it has been replaced for independence and choosing how one would live out one's life.

The only remaining problem with the rise of the independent self is when reality strikes and the inevitable occurs where the elderly begin to lose their independence through serious illness or infirmity. This gives rise to the question: If independence is what we live for, what do we do when it can no longer be sustained?

The inevitable soon began for Alice Hobson after she turned eighty-four. She started experiencing falls and memory issues, although she suffered no broken bones during these falls, the doctor the family brought her to had no answers for her issue as there was no fixable problem. Alice was unsteady, her memory was declining and these issues were only going to increase for her. The doctor could provide no answers, direction or guidance, and not even a prediction of what to expect next.

2 – THINGS FALL APART

For most of history each day was a roll of the dice. It didn't matter if you were six or sixty, death could happen instantly at any time for any reason even if life was puttering along at a nice steady state. With medical progress and improved sanitation, death from disease or trauma has been greatly reduced, especially in early childhood.

We all die of something eventually however. Even though modern medicine has found ways to stave off the inevitable for many diseases long after the initial diagnosis, the inevitable always occurs. For many people, they get to live a full life before old age claims them. Of course something must be written as the cause of death on their death certificate, but the reality is that there was no single cause that led to their death. People's bodily systems start failing, we perform patch jobs here and there, control the disease, or replace the joint until the body gradually gives out. The curve of life instead of being a nice steady state that instantly drops off from a peak, has now become a long, slow descent. Two major results of the advances in modern medicine has been the biological transformation that has changed the course of our lives and has also created a cultural transformation of how we think about the course of our life, in particular, the ending stages.

The story of aging is the story of our bodily organs. Our teeth, gum, jaws, bones, and blood vessels all degrade as or body ages and this results in either limited ability to function or causes our body to work harder to function. For example, at the age of thirty the brain is a three pound organ that barely fits in our skull. By our seventies there is almost an inch of room separating our brain from our skull due to loss of gray-matter in our brains. The frontal lobes of the brain responsible for judgement and planning are the first to shrink, this is followed by the hippocampus where memory is organized. Even though the slow deterioration of our body can be slowed through diet and physical activity, it cannot be stopped. Eventually our functional lung capacity decreases, our bowels slow down and our glands stop functioning.

Why we age has been something scientists, philosophers, and researchers have been debating for decades. The classical view on aging argues that we are like any complex system. We fail gradually through random wear and tear. The latest and newest view argues that aging is more orderly and is genetically programmed. Gawande argues that if the latter were the case for aging however, why it would be that in our short history the average life expectancy has been as low as twenty-eight years and has since substantially increased. It actually turns out genetic inheritance has little influence on longevity, as low as only 3 percent as noted by James Vaupel, of the Max Planck Institute for Demographic Research in Germany. Even genetically identical twins vary wildly in life span with the typical gap being more than fifteen years.

Following on from the gradual and random wear and tear model, as with any complex system, they function reliably until a critical component fails, this critical component in our bodies are our organs which luckily have fail-safes. We have backup systems, and sometimes even backup systems to the backup systems in our bodies. For example we have an extra kidney, an extra lung, and extra copies of a gene if one fails. But eventually we wear down until we can no longer function when a critical component fails us.

People prefer to avoid the subject of aging. And any book titles covering the subject tend to lean towards defying reality and instead avert our attention to other topics such as how to become more youthful. Due to medical advances, there has been what's called a "rectangularization" of survival as a larger percentage of the population has shifted to older ages. In the past, many populations would be very bottom heavy with children making up a larger share of the population thus having more of a triangle structure when it came to age demographics.

In 1950, those over the age of eighty made up 1% of the population. In thirty years time, there will be as many people over eighty as there are under 5 years of age. What is frightening about this is that people are putting less money aside in their savings now for old age than they did since the Great Depression. More than half of the elderly have no spouse and we are also having fewer children than we did before decreasing our chances of family taking care of us. There has virtually been no thought as to how we will live out our later years alone.

Even though the aged population has increased exponentially due to medicine and has caused dramatic changes in population demographics, medicine has been slow to confront these changes it has been responsible for. The number of certified geriatricians (doctors specialized and dedicated to the art and science of managing old age) between 1996 to 2010 in the United States has decreased 25% during this period of time. There isn't as much money in geriatrics in comparison to plastic surgery and truthfully, a lot of doctors don't like taking care of the elderly. The elderly are hard of hearing meaning you must be patient with them, some have multiple chief complaints, and the issues you are dealing with aren't necessarily fixable problems due to the chronic issues these patients face.

As a geriatric doctor it is important for the patient's feet to be examined. They need to be inspected carefully inch by inch, from the bottom of their soles, to the tip of their toes. This is because the most serious threat and danger the elderly face is usually a fall resulting in a broken hip that may land them in a nursing home or without the ability to ever walk again.

The three primary risk factors for falling are poor balance, taking more than four prescription medications, and muscle weakness. The elderly that don't have any of these three risk factors have a 12 percent chance of falling in a year, those with all three have a 100 percent chance. Gawande observed several geriatric doctor and patient consultations, at the end of these consultations the geriatric doctor stated that the job of any doctor was to support quality of life and this meant two things: (1) to provide as much freedom from disease as possible and (2) the ability to function for active engagement in the world. In Gawande's experience however, most doctors simply treated the disease and paid no attention to the rest believing that it will take care of itself. And if it doesn't, if the patient is becoming infirm or heading for a nursing home – well, then it's not a medical problem for the doctor is it? To a geriatrician, though, it is a medical problem.

Alice's doctors never took her falls as a warning sign that changes needed to be made so that her independence could be maintained. As matters got worse, Alice was in a car accident that could have ended really badly as she backed up all the way into the bushes of the neighbor's house across the street. For everyone there comes a tipping point when one realizes things are no longer the same, for Alice it was the tree trimmer scam that was pulled on her that brought Alice's family around to make the decision to visit retirement communities. Tree trimmers she had hired for a job told her she had to pay a thousand dollars for the work they did. They cornered her in her house and kept after her till she eventually paid them the fee. Then they came back the following day arguing for another seven thousand dollars. In the end she paid them again but this time the neighbors had heard the arguing and got the cops involved. The scam artists were caught and put in prison but it didn't make Alice any happier, because now she was looking at having to move into retirement communities, which she wanted no part of and as such, she was on the path to losing her independence.

In a year, less than 300 doctors will complete geriatrics training and this isn't nearly enough to replace the doctors that will retire, let alone reach the numbers required for the amount of elderly people coming through in the next decade. Chad Boult, a geriatrics professor, suggests that the remaining alternative would be to direct geriatricians toward training all primary care doctors and nurses in caring for the old, instead of providing the care themselves. This is a tall order however as only 97% of medical students ever take a course in geriatrics.

3 – DEPENDENCE

As we age it's not death that we fear, it's the aging process. It's losing our memories, our hearing, our loved ones, and becoming dependent on others to take care of us. We know this is what is coming for us down the road and we just don't want to face it. As fewer of us experience sudden deaths with medical advances, this means that most of us will spend greater periods of our lives in reduced and debilitated states depending on others to live. No one likes to think about this, especially if they're going to be placed in the situation, as a result most of us are unprepared for it.

Alice was afraid of leaving her home and dreaded giving up her independence, but she was resigned to it after the scam that had been pulled on her. Her family looked for a nice place that was close by and affordable. They found a place where she could have her own room and her own things and even hired a decorator to put everything in its place. But to Alice all this meant was that she had lost her home. And the same day she moved into her new place, she parked her car in the wrong parking lot and realized that she shouldn't be driving anymore. On the same day, Alice lost her car and her home.

Since moving to her assisted living home Alice did not seem happy at all, nor did she seem to adjust to her new living arrangements. She stopped cooking for herself, stopped eating as much, kept to herself, and didn't partake in any of the activities offered. Gawande noticed the light had gone out from behind her eyes although she remained recognizably herself, she had withdrawn. Her family took her to see a doctor who put her on medication to help, but it didn't help. Her life had changed drastically and she had no say or control about it.

Back in the early 1900's, unless the family could take the elderly in, the elderly were resigned to "poorhouses" or "almshouses" for shelter. This is where the frail, disabled, and diseased would be housed when they had no alternative options. The places were filthy, ridden with bed bugs, rats, flies, the odor of urine, and disease ran rampant throughout these shelters. Needless to say, there was a lack of basic physical care for those sheltered here. Fortunately, the industrialized world's elderly have escaped this alternative as it was phased out over time. Yet funnily enough, many still consider modern old age homes frightening, desolate, and grim places to spend the last phase of one's left.

Alice's assisted living home was nothing like a poorhouse. However, she never got used to living there despite all the facilities, support and care provided to her by the staff and her family. The place only grew more intolerable for her and with each passing day she became more miserable. Alice didn't know why she was so unhappy, the best way she could explain it was that it just didn't feel like home to her. Alice was taken to a place where people would take care of her but she didn't want to be taken care of. She wanted to live her life the way she wanted to, and that independence was stripped from her due to the structure and supervision she had to adhere to, which was more than she had ever faced when she lived by herself. Giving up her home meant giving up the life she had built for herself over many years.

To understand our system today, we have to go back in history and see how it all unraveled beginning with the poorhouse and what we eventually substituted them with. A poorhouse wasn't viewed as an issue by society back then, it was viewed as a medical problem that could be fixed so people were taken out of these institutions and placed in hospitals. The modern nursing home evolved from this, more or less by accident.

From World War II onwards, hospitals boomed and most people had access to a hospital that was nearby. There were all kinds of breakthroughs coming out in medicine such as antibiotics and blood pressure medications. We learned how to do transplants and this made hospitals the place to be. As an abundance of hospitals were built they became the place to put the elderly, the infirm, and the disabled which put an end to the poorhouse. By the mid 1900's hospitals were getting overcrowded with patients with chronic illnesses that could not be solved. As a result separate facilities were built for those needing extended periods of time for recovery and they were called "nursing" homes because hospitals needed to clear out the hospital beds.

Soon enough, much like hospitals, nursing homes began emerging all over the country. As long as you were a facility deemed to be working towards meeting the standards set by the Bureau of Health Insurance you would be licensed to operate as a "nursing home". Thousands of nursing homes resulted from this and so did reports of neglect and mistreatment. It took a few years for regulations to be tightened, and safety laws to be enforced for nursing homes, however the health and safety problems were finally addressed. The core problem however still persists for the elderly.

These aged care patients would spend a year or more of their lives in an institution that was never truly made for them.

Soon Alice started experiencing frequent falls and after a few minor repercussions, she had a fall that landed her in the hospital with a broken hip that sent her to a nursing home. She had always vehemently refused to live in one but now she had no choice. She never recovered from her broken hip and was now confined to a wheelchair and this meant all her daily activities were now laid out for her by the hour. She had no say of when she got up, got dressed, ate her meals, or went to the toilet. All of Alice's privacy and control was stripped from her.

Erving Goffman, a sociologist, compared nursing homes to prisons. The two institutions including military training camps, orphanages, and mental hospitals were termed "total institutions" – places isolated from greater society. Goffman noted four characteristics shared by a total institution. Firstly, everything that occurs is done in the same place and under the same authority. Secondly, all activities are done in groups with other people who participate in the same things and are treated the same. Thirdly, the entire day is scheduled with one activity leading into the next which are all led by the same central authority. And lastly, the daily schedules are designed to fulfill the aim of the institution with no choice in the matter given to the people regimented to the daily schedule.

In a nursing home, the aim of the institution is to care for residents. The definition of caring that has evolved throughout time however has no direct connection to what most elderly residents would define as living. It would be a rare occasion in a nursing home for someone to sit down with you and try to figure out what living a life meant to you under the current circumstances you faced. This stems as a result of a society that ignores the

18

final phase of the human life cycle by trying to place it out of sight, and out of mind.

A few weeks after her hip fracture Alice's son, Jim, came over for a visit. Alice leaned over to her son and whispered "I'm ready". Her son understood and was saddened by this however made arrangements for a Do Not Resuscitate order to be put on record for Alice. A few months later after experiencing some abdominal pains Alice kept quiet and didn't call for the nurse. Alice just laid there and waited and endured. In the morning she was gone.

4 – ASSISTANCE

You would think protests and riots would have resulted from nursing homes but none of this has happened because many of us believe it's the best alternative for when we are old, weak, and too frail, especially if you can't live with any family.

Lou was eighty-eight when he and his daughter had a difficult decision to make about his future. After experiencing several falls and memory lapses they found out that Lou had Parkinson's and so was put on medications, but he still kept falling despite the medications. Having lived by himself up until this point he didn't want anything to do with a retirement or nursing home, so his daughter, Shelley, let him move in with her and her family. Both parties had to endure through an adjustment period under these new living arrangements as the parent and child traded roles.

Lou found ways to adapt and made friends with some unlikely people such as the mailman, an Iranian clerk at a video store, and a younger gentleman named Dave that Shelley prearranged to come over.

Unfortunately the falls did not stop occurring. The doctors took Lou off his Parkinson medications as they believed it may have been the cause, but this only made his tremors worse and put him on even more unsteady grounds. Eventually he was diagnosed with postural hypotension, a condition of old age where the body loses its ability to maintain a stable blood pressure. When he changed positions, such as from sitting to standing, his body was not able to maintain his blood pressure and this made him unsteady and more prone to falling. The doctors simply said to Shelley that she needed to be more careful with him.

There were other issues that Lou had however, for instance, he wouldn't wear protective disposable underwear, and with his prostate problems Shelley had to change his clothes frequently. He also didn't like the food Shelley made for her family so she had to start making separate meals for him. And because his hearing wasn't great he would play music at deafening levels. Shelley finally got him some earphones, he didn't necessarily like wearing them, but he did. Lou would also have night terrors resulting in him screaming and shouting in the middle of the night.

The demands grew greater and greater on Shelley over time, apart from working and being a mother, she also had to take care of Lou. She finally had an aged care nurse come out to assess the situation and the nurse told Lou that given his disabilities, and his increased needs, he needed more help than he was able to get at home. Shelley couldn't stop working so Lou had to look for an alternative place to stay. The first place they visited wasn't a nursing home, but rather an assisted living facility.

Assisted living is often regarded as an intermediate station between independent living and life in a nursing home. Keren Brown Wilson, one of the originators for the assisted living concept that began in the 1980's was attempting to eliminate the need for nursing homes completely through this concept. She wanted to make a place where the elderly could live and not feel as if they were a part of a regimented asylum but actually felt like they were at home. At home, the elderly could decide what they did, when they wanted to do something, how their space was arranged, where they were able to keep their own possessions, and decide and make choices for themselves. When Wilson went to gather support for the assisted living concept no one wanted to touch it. Finally she was able to find a private investor and went to the state of Oregon to apply for exemptions to make her concept into a reality. She spent many hours in government offices to secure the exemptions and was finally provided them.

Park Place opened in 1983 with 112 units that were filled with "tenants", none of the residents at Park Place were called patients. Each of the units were private apartments that had a kitchen, private bath, and a front door that could be locked (which many people found hard to imagine). Tenants could live with their pets, bring in their own furniture, and choose their own carpeting as if they were apartment dwellers. They were also provided extra help that the elderly with advancing disabilities needed that were similar to services provided at nursing homes. These services included on-site nurses, an emergency button they could push 24 hours a day, activities people their age enjoyed, and care providers that understood they were assisting the tenants in their homes. Most of all, the tenants were able to make their own decisions, even if those decisions went against doctor's orders.

The concept was attacked immediately by outsiders, many saw it as a dangerous means for the elderly to live. How do you care for someone who can lock their door on you? How do you care for the elderly who have the ability to smoke, cook, use sharp knives, and drink alcohol? How are you going to keep the rooms clean and free of bacteria and urine, especially with pets and the elderly who are prone to accidents themselves? Wilson was not offering simple answers but she held herself and her staff responsible for finding ways to ensure tenants' safety, while providing them their privacy and individual homes. The state monitored the experiment closely and when Wilson expanded to a second facility in Portland with 142 units she was required to document the health, cognitive capabilities, physical function, and life satisfaction of the tenants. When the results of the data came back, it was found that tenants' life satisfaction had increased, cases of major depression declined, physical and cognitive function had improved, and the cost for those on government support was actually 20% lower compared to nursing homes. Wilson's assisted living program turned out to be a remarkable success.

Wilson's work was an attempt to solve a simple puzzle: what makes life worth living when we are old, frail and dependent on others? Studies have shown that as people age they tend to spend more of their time with family and close friends and interact with fewer people that they have the greatest connection with. They also focus more on being, rather than doing things to keep themselves busy, and are concerned with the present more so than the future. Laura Carstensen, a Stanford psychologist, has led research studies that have shown this course of actions results due to a matter of perspective.

As we age we begin to appreciate the relationships we have and the everyday simple pleasures. We begin to realize that we only have so long in this world and we want to enjoy the finite time that we have left. When we are young we tend to believe we will live forever and so we are willing to delay gratification for the future. We invest our time in developing our skills and resources for a brighter future, we try to meet more people, expand our networks, and tap into streams of knowledge and information. As we begin to see the future as finite and uncertain however, we shift our focus to the here and now, to everyday pleasures and to the people closest to us.

Wilson's assisted living concept spread like wildfire and she began teaching others how to build more assisted living facilities. Other facilities began emerging all over the country, unfortunately developers started slapping the name on bastardized and watered-down versions of Wilson's original intent. Wilson had originally created assisted living to help people like her mother who were in the lower income demographic elderly using Medicaid. Unfortunately everyone wanted their piece of the pie, including Wilson's board of directors as they wanted to build bigger facilities in larger towns while she wanted to focus on building smaller facilities in little towns that had no alternative options to nursing homes. Her board of directors wanted the more profitable areas and Wilson wanted to help those in need. They kept arguing back and forth over a period of time until she finally stepped down as CEO and sold all of her shares. With the money she made she started a foundation in her mother's name to continue working on changing aged care with her husband.

Wilson explained that the success of the concept has resulted from tenants being able to maintain their sense of independence; she aimed to help tenants do as much for themselves as they could. If tenants weren't able to physically dress themselves, they should at least pick out their outfit and then be provided assistance to put their clothes on. Dressing someone is easier than letting them do it themselves, and it takes less time and aggravation, this unfortunately results in staff at other institutions dressing people like they are rag dolls. And that's how everything goes downhill, one activity gets taken away, then something else does, then everything is regimented and set to a schedule right down the line from morning till evening. With this mindset and culture in place, the actual tasks performed by the staff takes over and are the first priority, the people being helped come second.

Most Assisted Living facilities are now built to relieve the guilt of children that place their parents in these facilities and are not actually built with the elderly in mind. They are built with nice friendly looking hotel lobbies. On guided tours the staff show off their computer labs and exercise rooms, boast about the numerous trips and activities that are available which almost no one attends. These are all features designed to show children the great things on offer for their parents who are going to be the one's living there. And of course, above all, they sell themselves as safe places to live with all the safety precautions that they have in place, which is just what the children want to hear. It isn't only the child's fault however, the parents are partly responsible as well because they give their decision making over to their children. It's rare for children to think in the shoes of their father and mother and consider if it would be somewhere they would enjoy living in. Instead, children tend to think in terms of "Is this a place I would be comfortable leaving Mom?"

Lou had only been in assisted living for a year before it was considered inadequate for his needs as his condition deteriorated. He kept experiencing falls yet refused to use a walker. As a result Shelley visited a nursing home nearby shortly after another severe fall and even though the nursing home looked horrible and was something that Lou never wanted to live in. Shelley felt she had to put him in there for his safety, because his safety came first above all. Even though he would hate it, she couldn't see another way.

Unfortunately this is the way it unfolds. In the absence of the ability for the family to care for the elderly at home, they are left with a controlled and supervised institutional existence, a medically designed answer to unfixable problems, a life designed to be safe but empty of anything residents truly cared about.

5 – A BETTER LIFE

In 1991 Bill Thomas was a new medical director of the Chase Memorial Nursing Home and he wanted to shake things up a bit. He saw despair everywhere he looked in the nursing home and it depressed him. He tried changing the patients' medications, but it didn't help. Thomas was fond of being self-reliant and was evident as he lived off the grid, grew his own food, used renewable energy sources for electricity and lived by the weather and seasons. Each passing day in the nursing home he realized that the residents had no independence so he decided to try and spice things up. He decided they needed to bring life into the nursing home to make a change.

Thomas had the kind of personality that could sell a hair dryer to bald men so he managed to sell his staff and superior on the idea he had for a different type of nursing home. Thomas considered the Three Plagues of nursing homes to be boredom, loneliness, and helplessness. To cure these plagues he believed life needed to be introduced into the nursing homes. He suggested placing living plants in every room, digging up the lawn and putting in its place a vegetable and flower garden and to bring in pets. Thomas wanted to bring in two dogs. They told him the code wouldn't allow for that. He said they'd just put it down on the paper. Then Thomas suggested an additional four cats, two for each floor. So they put it down. Then Thomas said one more thing was necessary, birds. Thomas didn't just want a few birds, he wanted a hundred birds. After a few more meetings and Thomas' skilled ability to sell ideas, he convinced the staff at the hospital to agree to the grant proposal that was to be submitted to the New York grant for innovations to fund the idea. Thomas then took a team to the state to lobby the officials for the proposal in person and the grant was eventually approved.

Thomas suggested that the proposal should not be implemented in piecemeal steps and instead and that it should instead be done all at once to disrupt the culture that was embedded into the nursing home. Every place has deep-seated cultures as to how things are done and Thomas wanted to shake this up at the nursing home.

They moved in two dogs, four cats, got rid of all the artificial plants and replaced them with real plants, and brought in a hundred birds all at once. Friends and family of the patients helped build a garden and a playground in the back of the nursing home for the kids. The hundred parakeets were delivered into the beauty salon without their cages as it hadn't arrived yet and the door was left shut. When the cages arrived the next day unassembled it was utter chaos but everyone came together, including the staff, residents, family and friends, to get the cages together and the birds were placed into their cages and were all delivered to various rooms.

It was amazing what happened! People believed to have lost their ability to talk began speaking and people who had completely withdrawn began joining in on activities such as taking the dogs out for a walk. The lights came back on in people's eyes. Researchers studied the effects of this program over two years and found that the number of prescriptions at the nursing home fell 50%, and even deaths fell by 15%.

As our time comes to an end we all seek comfort in simple pleasures such as companionship, good food, and sunlight on our faces. We are less ambitious but we still have a deep need to identify to a purpose that is outside ourselves. Something that will make living feel worthwhile and meaningful. Thomas chose animals, children, and plants for Chase Memorial Nursing Home as a medium for this and the program was called Eden Alternative.

The problem with medicine and the institutions that have been created to care for the sick and old are that they have taken no view at all on what it means for a life to be significant. Their focus has been much too narrow. They only view problems or diseases as things to be fixed and solved, and don't take into account the needs of the soul. The painful paradox of this is that we have allowed these institutions to decide and define how we live out our waning days. If safety and precaution was all we required in life, then the current system would be considered a success however because we seek more from life, to have meaning, worth and a purpose - it has failed to meet our needs.

A new retirement community called NewBridge in the Boston suburbs was one of the latest communities for elderly living attempting to address this issue. NewBridge was divided into pods housing no more than 16 people per pod. Each **pod** was built with private rooms based around a common area with a dining room, kitchen, and activity area. The households were designed to specifically avoid the look and feel of a clinical setting and to encourage social interaction between the residents. The open communal area encouraged people to see what others were doing and to allow them to join in. As a result there were more friendships and an increased sense of safety with residents still being able to maintain their privacy.

NewBridge shared their grounds with a private school that taught kindergarteners to eighth graders. Some of the residents would volunteer as tutors or librarians in their spare time at the school, and when students were studying World War II they would have the privilege of listening to firsthand accounts and stories from the residents. The residents attended the many art shows, musical performances, and plays put on by the students and middle schoolers even had a buddy program with the residents.

Providing meaning to elderly people is a new concept in today's society. It requires more imagination and creativity than making them merely safe to live out the rest of their lives. The solutions are not well defined yet however steps and measures are being taken to revolutionize industry practices and institutions.

Fortunately for Lou, someone informed Shelly about the Leonard Florence Center for Living. Each room was a single and this meant Lou could have his privacy again which was something he dearly wanted. This was an incarnation coming out of Bill Thomas' Eden Alternative program. This time Thomas wanted to make something from scratch, which he called the Green House, this eventually turned into the Green House Initiative that supported construction for 150 more centers throughout the country including the Florence Center where Lou was looking to live.

At the Florence Center, there were two wings on each floor that were called a Green House that housed ten people living together. Each resident had their own room centered around a large living room with ordinary furniture and a hearth. Residents were able to eat their meals around one big table together and Lou loved the center. He could do what he wanted, when he wanted, go where he wanted, wake up when he wanted, and go to bed when he wanted. There was no set schedule and no one telling him when to bathe and when to get dressed and when to do this or that. The frontline caregivers did the cooking, cleaning, and helped out with certain activities, and as a result the caregivers spent more time with the residents getting to know them, talking, playing cards, and participating in other activities with them.

The fear of old age and illness is not just the losses we will be forced to endure but it also includes the isolation we might face. As we become more fragile and realize our finitude, we don't want more money or more power. We just want to keep shaping the story of our life; to have the ability to make choices and deepen our connections with others. And this is all possible if the right place is found, and the right places are out there if you look hard enough.

6 – LETTING GO

Once Gawande had witnessed the shift occurring in how we treated our elderly, he wondered about the deep ramifications it may have toward medicine and current practices. A major insight he discovered was that as people's health waned, making their lives better actually might require stopping our purely medical endeavors for a second and to defy our urge to control and fix the situation. This raised the question: When should we try to fix the problem, and when should we not?

Sara Monopoli was thirty-four and pregnant with her first child when doctors at Gawande's hospital discovered she was going to die. It started with a cough and chest pains and when she arrived at the hospital the X-rays showed her left lung had collapsed and her chest was filled with fluid. It wasn't an infection as everyone had suspected, it was lung cancer. Her family was shocked as she had never smoked in her life. The next day Sara was induced into labor as per the doctors instructions so treatment could begin straight away, she delivered a healthy baby girl.

Sara's cancer was inoperable as it had metastasized to multiple lymph nodes in her chest and its lining. Chemotherapy was an option suggested for treatment so she began with a drug called erlotinib. Gawande notes that there is currently no cure for lung cancer and even with chemotherapy, the median survival length is roughly a year.

Three weeks after giving birth Sara was admitted to the hospital with shortness of breath that turned out to be a pulmonary embolism - a blood clot in an artery of her lung. She was put on blood thinners to help with this and further testing had shown that the chemotherapy drug she was on wasn't going to work for her. She was put on a second chemotherapy drug but by the end of the summer the results came back negative again as the tumors had grown. Sara tried her best to stay positive despite her cancer worsening. The third drug regimen she tried also hadn't worked and the cancer had spread even further now. Time was running out now and this led to the moment that posed the difficult question of what Sara and the doctors should now do? Or, to phrase it another way, what would you want your doctors to do?

This issue has garnered attention around the world as cancer costs worldwide has been documented to have a significant initial cost, if all goes well however, the cost tapers off as the cancer is managed over time. But for a patient whose cancer turns out to be fatal, their costs skyrocket and death eventually results anyway. This soaring cost of health care has become a major threat to economies of well developed nations.

In 2008 a national Coping with Cancer project published a study showing that ill cancer patients given extra life saving measures had a considerably worse quality of life in the last weeks of their life compared to those who did not receive the same measures. For those who were given the extra life saving measures it was found that their caregivers were three times more likely to suffer severe depression six months after the cancer patient had died. Because most of these cancer patients spend the majority of their final days in the ICU, they aren't able to say their goodbyes and arrange their affairs that would allow both the patient and family to depart peacefully.

People with serious illnesses have other needs than wanting to simply live longer. Surveys report that the most common concerns for the terminally ill are the avoidance of suffering, spending more time with family and close friends, being cognitively aware, not being a burden on others, and feeling that their life is complete. Medical care fails to meet these needs and the cost of this failure is measured in greater terms than mere dollars. The question is then not how can we afford this expensive system, but how can the health care system actually help people achieve what is most important to them at the end of their lives?

These days death comes after a long medical struggle through prolonged illness that is ultimately dire, or it comes from the normal wear and tear that aging brings. In these cases, death is a certainty however there is uncertainty placed around when the end will actually come and when one should acknowledge that the battle has been lost. The days of swift catastrophic illnesses are behind us and are now the exception rather than the rule. During a consultation with a patient's family that had recently undergone surgery, Gawande was asked if the patient was dying. Gawande wasn't even sure what "dying" meant anymore due to the technological advances medicine has made with the ability to sustain life of the 'dying' in vegetated states. Medical science and advancements in this field has created a new difficulty for mankind - knowing how to die.

On a Spring Friday morning, Gawande went on patient rounds with Sarah Creed, a hospice nurse at his hospital to learn more about hospice.

From what little he knew, he believed that hospice specialized in providing care for the terminally ill, sometimes at their hospital facilities, or at other times in the patient's home. For a patient to be emitted into hospice, a doctor has to write a note certifying the patient has less than six months to live. In Gawande's experience, many of his patients did not enter hospice as he believed the patients did not want to sign the form stating they understood their disease was terminal and that they would be giving up medical care that could give them a slight chance of living.

On the patient rounds they went to see a woman named Lee who had congestive heart failure. Creed asked Lee a series of questions about her pain, her breathing patterns, appetite and sleeping patterns, and any other discomforts she may have had. Creed made sure all of Lee's medical equipment was working and when a machine was in orderly fashion, she had emergency repairs called in straight away. Creed also checked on Lee's medications and when she discovered that some were missing because Lee had not been able to order more in she called Lee's pharmacy to have it sent over right away. The two then briefly chatted about the good days and Creed went over the procedure of what Lee should do if she started experienced any major pains.

Afterwards, Gawande admitted to Creed he was confused by what she was doing. He was under the impression that the goal of hospice was to let nature take its course. Creed explained to Gawande that the goal of hospice was to actually allow patients to live out the rest of their lives to their fullest ability possible in the present moment despite their severe disabilities. This meant the goal was to focus on patients being free from pain, staying mentally aware for as long as possible, or having outings with their family every once in a while. When Lee had entered hospice the doctors had given her less than a few weeks to live, but with hospice care she had already managed to live for a year.

Hospice is never an easy choice for a patient to make as only about a quarter of the patients entering hospice truly believe that they are going to die, despite being diagnosed with a terminal illness. Hospice is available to make sure patients have the right equipment in their home including medical beds, medications, and necessary support to aid them through the process such as physical therapy, occupational therapy, and a twenty-four-hour hospice nurse on call to provide instructions on what rescue medications to use in emergencies. Hospice offers a new ideal for how we can handle end of life situations.

But for Sara, this wasn't to be. She never considered hospice, she kept searching for solutions and tried any available option to fix her problem. She had said to her family that she wanted to spend her final moments at home surrounded by her family, and not in the hospital, but her final moments weren't something she or her family were ready to discuss yet. They just couldn't believe there wasn't something out there that could be done to cure her. Her doctor brought up the subject of supportive care but he soon got the signal from Sara and her family that they only wanted to talk about treatment options so he told them of an experimental treatment that may have a chance of helping.

Sara had to undergo a fourth chemotherapy drug to try and fix the pulmonary embolism before she could be let into the experimental treatment. Later that year Sara's cancer had spread to her spine, liver, and lungs. The pulmonary embolism was gone but new scans showed the cancer had now spread to her brain and the experimental treatment drug was not made to cross the blood-brain barrier, so the treatment would have no effect. But still her family was ready to battle the cancer till the very end, Sara kept trying different treatments and as time went by her health declined severely.

Three days before Sara was to begin a new round of chemo, her husband woke to find that Sara's skin was gray and she heaved heavily with each breath that she took. Her family brought her straight to the emergency room and she was diagnosed with pneumonia despite the safety precautions that her family had taken to avoid it. Unfortunately her immune system had weakened to the state that their precautions had not prevented the pneumonia. They pumped her with antibiotics and oxygen as her breathing became more difficult and her oxygen levels dropped. The next day she drifted out of consciousness and was moved into the intensive care unit.

In 2004 Aetna, an insurance company, attempted to try a different approach in minimizing hospital costs from terminally ill patients. Instead of reducing aggressive treatments, Aetna increased the incentives for policyholders to explore hospice options. Those with less than a year to live were also allowed to receive hospice while still receiving their treatments. They performed a two year study and found that those who enrolled in hospice increased from 26% to 70% of patients. And surprisingly those who enrolled went to the ER half as much as the people who weren't enrolled in hospice. Total hospital and ICU costs fell by two-thirds.

Aetna ran another broader study with terminally ill patients offering only hospice care, and enrollment again reached 70%. As a result hospital service use declined sharply, and use of ICUs went down by more than 85%. The real difference that resulted from these experiments was that patients were given someone who understood what they were going through and who were willing to listen and talk to the patients about what they wanted. The previous Coping with Cancer study reported that patients who enrolled in hospice also suffered less, were physically capable for longer, were able to interact with others, and their families were less likely to suffer from persistent depression after their loved ones had passed.

Through these studies it was evident that the terminally ill who had discussions with their doctor about their end-of-life preferences had a higher likelihood of dying at peace and in control of their situation which spared their family any additional anguish.

Our decision making in medicine has failed because we have reached the point of actively causing harm to patients through treatments that provide a minute chance of surviving as we don't want to confront the subject of mortality and what the patient really wants out of the end of their life. Patients who receive hospice or palliative care receive this, the rest don't. And oddly enough, for those who receive hospice care, they have been found to actually extend their lives beyond what their doctors thought would be imaginable.

Gawande consulted with a palliative care specialist, Susan Block, to discuss how he could better approach the topic of mortality with his patients. Block explained that most doctors go into the discussion trying to determine whether or not the patient wants them to fix the problem. But the real task doctors should be aiming for is to ease the patients' anxiety; their anxiety about possible death, about suffering, about how their loved ones are feeling, about being a burden to their loved ones, and about their finances. Patients have many worries, and it may take more than one conversation to get through to the heart of all their anxieties and to help them understand the limits of what medicine can and can't do for them.

The most important thing required is that doctors sit down with their patients and really take the time to understand where they are coming from and answer their questions, even the annoying questions. Block emphasizes that they must make the time, period. Doctors shouldn't be there attempting to determine which treatment is better, they should be finding out what is most important to the patient so they can provide advice on what can give them the best way of getting what they want out of the remaining time they have left. There are things they will want to achieve in their remaining time and doctors must try their best to help them achieve those goals. This requires both listening and talking. And the words you use matter, it is always better to ask "If time was to suddenly become short, what is most important to you?" rather than "What do you want when you are dying?"

Block runs through a list of questions with her patients before the time arrives when the life or death decisions must be made:

What does the patient understand about their prognosis?

What are their concerns about what lies ahead?

What kinds of trade-offs are they willing to make?

How do they want to spend their time if their health worsens?

And who do they want to make decisions on their behalf if there comes a time when they can no longer decide?

Sara had discussions about what she wanted, but not how her goals could be reached. Dr. Morris, Sara's primary care physician was concerned that the oncologist and the hospital weren't doing the best they could for Sara. He explained to the family that he was really worried about her. The cancer had made her severely weak and in her current state this made it even harder for her to fight off the infection from the pneumonia. He knew that nothing was going to stop the cancer, even if they were able to get the pneumonia under control. The family agreed that he should continue administering the antibiotics and call upon palliative care so that they could provide her with morphine to help ease her breathing and suffering. As a family they decided not to do anything else and by the next morning Sara had finally let go.

7 – HARD CONVERSATIONS

Doctors worldwide are all too ready to offer false hope that leads to families to empty their bank accounts and dip into their children's education funds for treatments that provide little hope of a solution to a terminal illness.

Scholars have proposed that there are three stages of medical development that countries go through that advances with economic development. The first stage is when poverty is the norm and most deaths occur in the household as there are little medical care facilities or accessibility available for the population. The second stage is when the economy is developing and people transition to higher income levels, more resources in the economy has led to widespread accessibility of medical facilities. People rely more on health care systems during this stage when they are ill and most people often die in the hospital instead of their home. The third stage occurs when the country's income climbs to the peak levels, people now have the privilege of worrying about the quality of their lives when they are ill or dying and deaths at home begin to rise again. This three stage process resembles the current progression the United States has made.

Hospice care has grown such that in 2010 45% of Americans died in hospice with more than half of the deceased receiving hospice care at home. Significant transformations are occurring in medicine and how the terminally ill are treated however we are currently stuck in a transitional phase. The institutionalized version of aging and death is slowly being phased out yet a new norm has not been established as of yet.

Gawande's father was in his seventies when he was faced with his own mortality. He started experiencing neck pains and slight numbing in his left hand so he went in for a checkup at the hospital. An X-ray showed that there was arthritis in his neck but after a few years had passed the pain increased and his whole hand was now becoming numb so he ordered an MRI and found that a tumor was growing inside his spinal cord. The tumor filled his entire spinal cord and extended all the way to the base of his brain.

Spinal cord tumors are not common and very few neurosurgeons have experience dealing with them. Gawande's family found two reputable neurosurgeons with experience in the field, one based in Boston and the other in Cleveland. Both surgeons offered surgery, but were careful to note that they could only remove a part of the tumor. The main goal of the surgery would be to provide more room for the tumor to grow by opening the spinal cord.

The neurosurgeon in Boston advised that surgery should be done right away as this was an extremely dire situation, if action was not taken quickly his father could possibly become a quadriplegic within weeks. Chemotherapy and radiation weren't options as they would not nearly be effective as surgery. The doctor in Cleveland offered the same surgery, but explained that spinal cord tumors don't usually advance rapidly and only progressed in stages with no rapid decline in health occurring. He advised that he saw no need for the surgery until his father felt the situation was unbearable and affected his life significantly.

Gawande's father was fearful of the tumor and what it was doing to him, but he was also fearful of the surgery. He asked multiple questions about the operation including how they cut the spinal cord open, what they did to cauterize the blood vessels, why they didn't use a different instrument he used in his practice, and many others. The Boston neurosurgeon said the tumor his father had was dangerous and that he had a lot of experience with these kinds of tumors. He left Gawande's father the ultimatum of either doing the surgery or not doing it. Right then his father has decided the Boston doctor was not for him.

The Cleveland doctor, Edward Benzel, understood that Gawande's father was more fearful of the procedure than of the tumor itself. So he answered his father's questions and asked some himself to better understand the situation. His father wanted to be able to continue practicing surgery for as long as possible which Benzel could relate to. Benzel believed his father could wait and see how his symptoms progressed and should hold off on the surgery until his father felt he really needed it. Benzel made further efforts to find out what Gawande's father truly desired and what he cared about. As time went on there was no change in symptoms even though subsequent MRI's showed that the tumor had grown. The decision was made to hold off on the surgery and to wait till things became direr.

There are 3 kinds of relationships doctors have with their patients. The first is a paternalistic relationship where the doctor aims to ensure the patient gets what the doctor believes is the best care possible. It's the doctor-knows-best way of thinking.

The second type of relationship is the informative. In the informative relationship the doctor provides the patient all of the available facts and lets the patient decide on what the best course of action would be. The doctor has the knowledge and the skills to do what is necessary but will leave the decision making to the patient.

The third type of relationship is interpretive. The interpretive relationship is where the doctor helps the patient decide what they want by asking the important questions. The questions discover what the patient truly values with questions such as "What is most important to you?" "What are your worries?" When the doctor discovers the answers they then explain which option could best serve the needs of the patient and help them towards achieving their priorities.

Gawande finally realized how understanding that the end of your life was near could be a gift. After his father's diagnosis, he noticed that he continued living as he had previously done so with his work, his tennis, his charities; however he also narrowed his focus and altered his desires. He made more time for family, visited his grandchildren more often and fit in an extra trip back to India to visit his relatives. Two and a half years after he was diagnosed his symptoms began to change. He started experiencing greater tingles and numbness in both his hands and would unexpectedly lose his grip on items. A few weeks later he made the decision to retire from surgery.

After retirement he threw his life into being Rotary district governor and took to the road with his wife as he aimed to speak twice at each of his district's 59 Rotary clubs. As he was visiting these clubs his strength kept waning, and he stopped by to visit Gawande in Boston. Gawande's father was worried he was going to be paralyzed and would soon become a burden on his wife. Gawande mustered up the courage and asked his father the important questions Block had suggested should be asked. His goals were to finish his Rotary duties and district governor term which was going to last two more months. He also wanted to ensure the college in India he had built and his family was going to be all right. His father said a life of paralysis was unacceptable for him and that he wanted to be able to function while living out the rest of his life. If he had the choice of being a quadriplegic or die, he said he would rather die. From there the decision was made to undertake the surgery as soon as his duties at the Rotary Club were finished.

Early into the surgery there were problems as Gawande's father was experiencing abnormal heart rhythms. Benzel stopped the surgery and came out to ask the family whether he should continue or stop. Gawande simply asked if his father would still be able to function if the surgery continued on, Benzel answered in the positive and as per his father's request told Benzel to continue. The surgery was a success. Gawande's father went into ICU for a couple days, and then went through rehabilitation for three weeks. He'd ultimately made the right choice to wait and do the surgery only when the tumor had become unbearable.

Life is filled with choices however, once you have made one there is another that must be made right around the corner. The tumor biopsy showed that Gawande's father had a slow-growing cancer and Benzel referred him to a radiation oncologist and a neuro-oncologist, unfortunately neither of these doctors were interpretive doctors like Benzel. They both advised him that treatment could retain his abilities and maybe even restore some. Gawande's father was clear about what he wanted but his doctors pushed him to get the treatment. They focused on all the upsides and explained that there would be minimal side effects from treatment, even

Gawande pushed him to go for the treatment as all he could see were benefits from taking the treatment.

Eventually Gawande's father opted for the treatment and they made a mold of his body where he would lay and not move for up to an hour to receive the treatment. This was tolerable at first, but over time, his back and neck started experiencing spasms and the position became harder and harder to endure. The radiation left him nauseous and with throat pains, the drugs he took to mitigate these effects just made him tired and constipated. Eventually he also lost the ability to taste food, the doctors never explained that this was a possibility and said it would come back after several weeks although it would never come back. By the time the radiation was over he had shooting pains throughout his arm, no sense of taste, and a constant ringing in his ears. He had also lost twenty-one pounds over the six weeks.

After six months they found that the tumor had expanded and his symptoms had only gotten worse. When they went in to discuss alternative chemotherapy treatments with the oncologist, the oncologist went into information mode and listed eight or nine options, none of which were to do nothing. Gawande's father questioned if the drugs would make his symptoms worse, she said it might, but this depended on the drugs he would take. There were too many options, too many risks and benefits to consider. His father left the consultation uncertain of what action to take.

Soon he began experiencing falls as his legs started experiencing numbness and this scared him, yet he still could not make a decision. Gawande went to visit his father and broached the topic of home hospice as an alternative option. His mother didn't believe it was necessary but his father said it wasn't a bad idea so they called someone out to explain what they could offer. A hospice nurse came over the following day and explained that under hospice care staff would help adjust his medications to minimize his nausea and make him less groggy. They offered services such as regular nursing visits, along with 24 hour emergency nursing support as required. He'd also be provided with fourteen hours of a home health aide to help with the basics of cleaning, grooming, bathing, and anything non-medical related. There would even be a social worker and a spiritual counselor available if he wanted, he could also drop the hospice services at any time. Gawande's father decided to start hospice care immediately.

The nurse then talked about a Do Not Resuscitate order and asked if he had a way to call a caregiver such as a bell or baby monitor, and also asked about his funeral arrangements. Gawande's father responded with no hesitation and it was evident he had already given thought to the subject much to the surprise of Gawande. They discussed what his biggest concerns were and he explained that he simply wanted to be able to stay in contact with his friends and family around the world via email and Skype. He didn't want to experience pain or suffering, and wanted to be happy.

The nurse told Gawande's father to stop experimenting and changing the doses of his drugs, and to always have someone available to help when he tried to get up from sitting down. Hospice ended up hiring a personal care aid to stay overnight to help him get to the bathroom at night. After that, there were no more falls, and they realized that every day without a fall reduced the pain he experienced and he even gained back some of his strength. Soon enough, Gawande's father was able to begin walking assisted with a walker for short distances. As Gawande gave the graduation address at his alma mater Ohio University, his father was able to attend and walk a short distance to watch his son provide the speech in the stands amongst everyone else. No one thought he'd ever be able to do what he did, but through hospice he was able to regain his strength which made it all possible.

8 – COURAGE

There are at least two types of courage required in aging and sickness. The courage to confront the reality of mortality and the courage to seek out the truth of what is realistic and what isn't. The most daunting is the second type of courage, the courage to act on the facts and truth of the end. The problem we face then is to decide whether our fears or our hopes are what should matter the most in making the right decision.

For most patients, having multiple treatment options simply overwhelms them and provides no value. Doctors must remember that they need to step back and stop playing Dr. Informative and ask the important questions from their patients. What are your greatest fears and concerns? What goals are most important to you? What trade-offs are you willing to make and which ones are you not? Not everyone is able to answer these questions.

For Gawande's patient, Jewel Douglass, she wanted to be without pain, nausea, and vomiting. And most of all she wanted to be able to be at her best friend's wedding which was just two days away. Her ovarian cancer had grown and multiplied and partially obstructed her intestines causing her abdomen to be filled with fluid. The options were chemotherapy and this would not get her to the wedding in time so that was ruled out; this answer also excluded any other type of surgery. As a result it was decided they would drain the fluid out of her abdomen and told her not to drink anything thicker than apple juice and to come back for treatment after the wedding. Douglass wouldn't make it to the wedding. She was back that same night vomiting again after her symptoms worsened. Given the circumstances, Gawande and Douglass agreed that surgery would be the best option however she was hesitant of proceeding as she didn't want to take any risky chances with surgery.

The Nobel Prize winning researcher, Daniel Kahneman, led a study on how we evaluated experiences related to pain and suffering and determined the "Peak-End rule". This rule stated that the amount of pain we experienced was determined by only two moments. The single worst moment of the procedure and the very end. So if the end of a procedure was relatively pain free, the participant that faced horrendous pain in the middle would evaluate the pain was not as bad as it actually was. However, if the pain at the end was excruciating, the entire experience would be remembering as being more painful. It was found that patients largely ignored the duration of pain and simply averaged these two moments. Several studies were undertaken after this and confirmed the Peak-End rule showing that we neglect the duration of suffering.

Gawande realized from the Peak-End rule that Douglass' fear was that she did not want to take a gamble on how her story would end. From Douglass' answers Gawande then suggested he should operate in a conservative manner, he would go in and look around, if he could unblock her intestines easily he would do so. If he could not however, he wouldn't go for it and would just put in tubes to drain her fluids. He would not take any risky chances with the operation. Douglass agreed with this approach and when Gawande went into surgery he saw that he could not easily unblock her intestines so that she could eat again, so he didn't take any risky chances, put in the draining tubes and closed her up. After the surgery Jewel Douglass had two weeks to say goodbye to her family and friends before she passed quietly in her sleep.

No one has full control of their life, call it fate, luck, or destiny, physics and biology have their way of intruding into our lives. With that being said however, we aren't left helpless either and this is something we must acknowledge with courage to recognize both of these realities. We have the ability to shape the end of our lives, though as we age, the effect of this ability decreases steadily. Our most cruel failure however is the failure to comprehend that the elderly have desires other than simply staying safe and living longer. We must realize that the elderly want the chance to shape the ending of their own lives and that we have the opportunity in our institutions and culture to alter the possibilities for them to live out their last chapter the way they want to.

Questions arise about how far those possibilities should go. Assisted suicide is something that is always brought up. At the root of the issue, the real argument is about the mistakes we fear making, the mistake of either prolonging suffering or shortening valued life. For the terminally ill, who we know will only live longer for more and more suffering; it's hard not to be sympathetic. But at the same time Gawande is less worried about assisted suicide being abused rather than the dependence that may come from it. Our ultimate goal is not a good death but a good life to the very end. With assisted suicide a dangerous belief may be reinforced with it that reducing suffering and improving lives through other means is not possible when one is infirm or terminally ill. Assisted living is much harder than assisted death, but its possibilities are also far greater for the sickly or old.

Eventually Gawande's father passed away and the family wasn't prepared for it despite their preparations. Hospice had made his situation manageable. Weeks went by that were good, and then months went by that were good enough. Each day Gawande's father found moments worth living for. It seemed like he could continue in this manner a long time but in retrospect there were signs he would not, his weight continually dropped, his medication dosages were increasing and Gawande even began receiving emails from him that he couldn't understand.

One night his father took a whole tablet of a narcotic pill instead of a half pill like he'd normally take because of the pain he was experiencing, and the next day his wife could not wake him. She called 911 instead of hospice because he was turning blue. His oxygen levels were low and an X-ray showed that pneumonia was present in his right lung and the situation seemed dire. As Gawande was sitting at the airport waiting to board his plane to see his father, his father remarkably awakened and lived for a further four days. It was hard to achieve but he was released from the hospital and was able to make it back home. Even in his last couple of days he could still experience some of the simple pleasures. He could still eat and talk to his grandchildren by phone, and even provided instructions on his unfinished projects. But during his last two days he was also in and out of consciousness a lot.

On his last day he said he didn't want to experience this anymore. He said that when he was asleep he was free of pain and had no worries. His anxieties and confusion would disappear, but then he would wake up and it would all come rushing back. What he wanted most of all at the end of his life was peace. In the late afternoon he stopped breathing and he was gone.

EPILOGUE

Being mortal is about our attempts to cope with our confinement of being human and having limits set by our genes, cells, flesh and bone. Science has given us the ability to test these limits and extend our lives, but at the same time, medicine has failed to admit that their power to save our lives is limited and always will be.

People believe that those in medicine only have the duty of ensuring health and survival. But there is so much more to it than that. The real duty is to sustain well-being and well-being is all about why one wishes to stay alive. The reason one wants to be alive doesn't just matter at the end of life, or when a debilitating illness comes, but all throughout life as well.

The vital questions one should ask when serious sickness or injury strikes are always the same. What is your understanding of the situation and its potential outcomes? What are your fears and what are your hopes? What are the trade-offs you are willing to make and not willing to make? And what is the course of action that best serves this understanding? Palliative care emerged to provide this kind of care to dying patients fortunately however palliative care is also being extended to those who are not only dying but to those who have debilitating illnesses as well. This however is not a cause for celebration, but a cause for encouragement. Celebrations can be warranted once all clinicians apply similar thinking to every patient they care for.

Gawande never expected that his most meaningful experiences as a doctor would come from helping others deal with the things that medicine couldn't help with as well as what it could. Gawande felt he was lucky and is forever grateful that he was able to hear his father's last wishes and to say goodbye. He knew his father was at peace in the end and that allowed him to be at peace as well.

CONCLUSION

Thank you for reading our Book§Swift Executive Summary on Atul Gawande's – Being Mortal, if you enjoyed this summary please leave a review by going to: http://**amzn.to/1GD3hHj**.

Also, if you would like to purchase the original *"Being Mortal: Illness, Medicine, and What Matters in the End"* by Atul Gawande, we highly encourage you to do so by going here: **http://amzn.to/1NcFS4k**.

FREE BONUS AND CONCLUDING NOTES

To claim your free bonus – How to Read a Book in One Day – head on over to: http://bit.ly/BSwiftBonus.

You can also check out our catalogue of Book§Swift Executive Summaries by visiting our Amazon Author page. We are continuously expanding our catalogue and would love to hear any requests you may have! Please contact us at summaryswift@gmail.com with any requests, feedback or questions.

Happy readings!

The Book§Swift Team

What to Do When You

A Kid's
Guide to
Overcoming
Anxiety

Huebner, Ph.D.

23138923R00041

Made in the USA
Middletown, DE
17 August 2015